JESUS
IN THE
ROOM

*A man headed for death
asks God to let him live so he can minister to others.*

MARY JO MOSHER
WITH GOD AND
LLOYD KOENIG

WESTBOW
PRESS®
A DIVISION OF THOMAS NELSON
& ZONDERVAN

WestBow Press books may be ordered through booksellers or by contacting:

WestBow Press
A Division of Thomas Nelson & Zondervan
1663 Liberty Drive
Bloomington, IN 47403
www.westbowpress.com
844-714-3454

Scripture quotations taken from The Holy Bible, New International Version® NIV® Copyright © 1973 1978 1984 2011 by Biblica, Inc. TM. Used by permission. All rights reserved worldwide.

ISBN: 979-8-3850-2907-5 (sc)
ISBN: 979-8-3850-2908-2 (e)

Library of Congress Control Number: 2024914268

Print information available on the last page.

WestBow Press rev. date: 07/30/2024

CONTENTS

ACKNOWLEDGMENTS

From the family: We're grateful for all the people who have prayed for us. The people at church, our prayer team, and Pastor Gerry and his family, who were helping us around the clock with everything that to us was overwhelming. That made a big difference with all that we were going through at that time.

From the author: Thanks also to others who made this book possible: Lloyd, who kindly gave me this opportunity and worked with me to make it happen; his wife Vicki, who supported him; daughter Katie, nurse Christie and other nurses; and anyone else who was part of this story, its purpose being to reveal the greatness of God, glorify Him, and save souls. Without all those people contributing, the book would not exist.

This book is dedicated to our Lord and Savior, who paid the price that we may live. To Him, we owe everything.

PREFACE

Even with a small congregation, it's difficult to get to know everyone. We may just know them in passing on our way into the church or out. That's the way it was for a published author who had belonged to the church for many years and didn't know Lloyd well. In 2023, her husband, who had been fighting cancer for some time, finally succumbed.

When he passed, she considered it a nightmare, and desperately wanted to join him. Each day for a long while, she went through the motions of living, praying for God to take her. Until one evening, she prayed, "I have no purpose anymore, so if you don't have anything for me to do for you, I want to join my husband."

A month or so later when the church service was over, Lloyd, who was sitting in his wheelchair, motioned her to come talk to him. "I suppose you know I had a stroke a couple of years ago."

"I heard that. Yes," she answered.

"Well, God performed many miracles when it happened, and I want you to write a book about it so others will become believers. And I don't want it to be about me," he insisted. "I want this book to glorify God because He's done so much for me, and I want people to know what He can do for them if they have faith in Him."

At first, the woman said, "I'm not sure I can, but I'll think about it. You can't find someone else who can do it?"

"No. I want you to do it."

"Why?"

"Because I know you can."

A couple of weeks later, the woman decided she would write it because she didn't want to disappoint Lloyd. Doubting her own capabilities, she told him if God would help her, she would do it. Because, without Him, she wouldn't succeed. She also realized this was God's answer to her prayer for giving her a purpose, and she didn't want to disappoint Him either. After that, Lloyd began gathering information about his stroke and dictated it to the author. It was written in late 2023 through the beginning of 2024.

INTRODUCTION

In the beginning was the Word, and the Word was with God, and the Word was God. He was with God in the beginning. Through Him all things were made; without Him, nothing was made that has been made. In Him was life, and that life was the light of all mankind.

JOHN 1-5

With God, anything is possible, even miracles. If that were not true, the universe and everything that exists wouldn't be here. He's the only one, with the help of His pollinating team, who can turn a beautiful flower into a cucumber, an apple, or any other kind of fruit or vegetable. When looking down on us at our mountain of grief, He makes the sun shine again, heals our bodies and much more, if we trust in Him, for there is purpose in everything He does.

Believing in Him isn't just knowing Jesus as a man who once walked on Earth, but knowing Him as our Lord and Savior, and having a relationship with Him through prayer and studying His Word to learn what He expects of us. It's committing our lives to Him and doing our best to follow in His footsteps. It's about doing what we know in our hearts is right rather than giving in to what we know is wrong because, otherwise, we might risk losing a friend or a job. In life, it's not about pleasing others; it's about pleasing God our father. It's about daily prayer, believing in healing through the laying on of hands, the power of the Holy Spirit, and miracles.

This is a story, not so much about the persons living it, because there aren't many people, including Jesus in His suffering at the hands of wicked people, who haven't experienced trials in their lives. Rather, it's about the greatness of God who helps us through them if we're wise enough to seek His help. God calls for us to be patient because He is patient and faithful. His answers to prayer don't always come immediately, sometimes not for years.

But we should never give up. God always answers prayer; it just happens when His time is right, and His answers are never without reason. We must be faithful in His Word and "Be still and know that I am God."

Many people ask that, if God is Love, as the Bible and those who believe in Him proclaim, why does he let bad things happen to good people who love Him and are obedient? Why is there so much suffering in this world? Lacking an answer or an understanding about who God is, there are people who immediately become angry, put the blame on Him and defy His existence instead of looking for the truth.

This story isn't about the man, but about how in the worst of times, a trust in Jesus resulted in not just one, but several miracles and turned trials into opportunities. It's about a God who loves His people, a God who cries with them, a God who knows what's best for them, who has a plan for those who believe and follow in his footsteps, a God who won't let you down.

That same man who, though he was facing death or permanent handicap, never gave up on God. He knew God's abilities were limitless and prayed every day for the miracles that would bring recovery. He was also aware that Jesus was by his side day and night because He promised He would always be with us.

This man wants others to know what happened because he is concerned about the people who won't be standing at the doorway of heaven as they face death; unless they turn from their sins and believe and trust in Him, not just in words, but in their hearts.

1

THE BEGINNING

God has put the body together, giving greater honor to the parts that lacked it, so that there should be no division in the body but that its parts should have equal concern for each other. If one part suffers, every part suffers with it. If every part is honored, every part rejoices with it.

1 CORINTHIANS 12:24-26

Oakwood's people, as in other churches, are often referred to as family because, as believers in Christ, they are children of God, and as such, brothers and sisters in Christ. They carry their church with them in prayer and service to our Lord, helping those in need and protecting their church family. Especially at a time when bad people full of hate and evil intent carry guns and turn against places of worship, destroying their buildings and killing worshipers.

To some, Lloyd at times seemed intimidating and aloof, sitting with his back against the foyer wall every Sunday morning studiously watching people come and go, conversing with some, ignoring others because he had a job to do. Most people knew his purpose and the kind heart that was tucked under his shirt, safely hidden along with the weapon that would protect his charge.

Not many were aware of the gun beneath his shirt and didn't need to know. Nor did they have to know there were others secretly carrying also. The pastor, who had a plan for emergencies, condoned and encouraged it because he trusted these people would know when and how to use them, praying they wouldn't have to, and that there was safety in numbers.

Though Lloyd knew them well, he didn't draw his strength from the gun. He drew his strength from his trust in God, his vow to follow in His footsteps, and his church family, most of whom had also placed their lives in Jesus' hands. It was a strength he passed on to his family and others, but would desperately need for himself in the coming years when it seemed his life and the lives of those closest to him had fallen apart.

Through it all, he knew God was with him because Jesus had said he would never leave anyone who had faith in Him no matter what happened in their lives. Lloyd's life, aside from Jesus, was his wife, two daughters, and three young grandchildren who depended on the head of the family to always be there for them as well.

Lloyd, like others, took his faith seriously. He walked and talked with Jesus every day through prayer and His Word, which told Lloyd what Jesus expected of him. Through these things, Lloyd had long ago promised to give up the sins of his past, never to go back, and embrace a new and rewarding life (be born again) following His will for him, and doing his best to be an example for others.

One day, while at church, a friend came up to Lloyd and asked, "Lloyd, when did you become saved?" So, Lloyd told him his story.

He was 29 and living in California when he became involved

with a church and attended Bible study every Wednesday afternoon. One day, the pastor, impressed with Lloyd's knowledge of the Bible but thinking something was missing, asked Lloyd to stay after Bible study ended and everyone had left.

"He pulled up an old rickety card table," Lloyd said, "and sat down across from me." Then he began talking about the Lord, wanting to know about Lloyd's faith.

"So, I told him, when I was nine years old and living in New Mexico, I never made Jesus my Lord. I never walked with Him, never followed Him. I just used Him like fire insurance, for lack of a better phrase."

"Lloyd, you're a good Bible student," the pastor told him. "I think deep down you love the Lord more than for insurance. Would you like to dedicate your life to Him? Follow Him and obey Him for the rest of your life? It doesn't mean life won't sometimes be difficult. But He'll always be there to walk you through it."

The pastor didn't have to wait long for an answer. The words were hardly out of his mouth when Lloyd said, "Of course, I do."

So, sitting at this old rickety, busted up card table, the pastor led Lloyd in prayer to put his life in the hands of Jesus.

"I've been doing this ever since that day." Lloyd said. "Praise God, it wasn't through a prayer of my own. My life and my heart belong to God."

Every day since then, like most believers, Lloyd begins each day thanking God for it. He also prays that, no matter what the day brings, he will be the example he needs to be for witnessing to others who may not know the Lord.

No one could predict what the future held for Lloyd and his family or anyone else, for that matter. Only God knew that. And Lloyd trusted Him.

Years later, what happened on a certain day wasn't planned.

It just began with prayer and progressed as usual from there. It wasn't anticipated, and it could have happened to anyone. When it did, he remembered the pastor from New Mexico telling him life won't always be easy just because you're a believer.

Later, when he had time to relive what had happened, Lloyd told his story to anyone who would listen, thinking it might give others hope through Jesus that they needed a sudden dark change in their lives such as he was going through. Because he knew that, as he walked with Jesus, anything was possible including miracles, and Lloyd trusted He would be with him all the way.

"He was and still is," Lloyd tells people.

2

WHAT HAPPENED

And we know that in all things God works for the good of those who love him. Who have been called according to His purpose.
ROMANS 8:28.

It was August 13, 2021 when Lloyd's need for Jesus became urgent.

It happened one warm sunny afternoon in August when people were walking their dogs, driving to the ice cream store, riding their bikes, or participating in some other outdoor activity. Because, soon children would be back at school, outdoor playtime would come to an end, and winter would be moving in.

That day, he had no knowledge of what was about to happen. He progressed with his day as usual that afternoon, stopping first at the local supermarket where he saw a woman at the checkout counter who knew Lloyd well. Beyond the usual greeting, the woman noticed he wasn't his usual talkative self and wondered if something was wrong.

"Maybe his mind is occupied today," the woman said to herself. "I have days like that too."

She left him to his thoughts as she checked him out and moved on to the next person in line. Neither one of them would have guessed something was going on that would permanently change his life and the lives of those closest to him.

When finished checking out, he picked up his package, said goodbye and continued on to the gym for his workout, unaware that it would be a day he would lean heavily on his God; a day when he would become totally helpless and could do nothing for himself. In an instant, and unexpectedly, his life would change while exercising at the gym in the small town of Becker, something he had often done in an effort to keep his gradually aging body physically strong.

After arriving at the gym, Lloyd walked in, greeted people he knew and began his workout. Finished with exercise in the weight room, Lloyd walked to the side of the room and sat down intending to take a short break before continuing.

"I always felt at home in the weight room," he said. "So, I just sat there taking in the activity that was going on."

He had sat a minute or two when something went wrong. There was no warning, no preparing for it, the pain in his head sudden and sharp, like lightning in a thunder storm. He tried to stand up and take steps. But he was unknowingly trying to fight off an invisible enemy; it just kept coming, gradually weakening him despite his efforts to win the battle. And it sent him to the floor before he could react, helpless, unable to move any part of his left side including his head.

"It sounded like someone broke one of those big pencils," he said, when someone asked what had happened. "You know, like they used in kindergarten, broke it in half, then shoved the pieces together and grinded them. I could hear the noise of the pencils breaking and the grinding inside my head. The pain was excruciating as I tried to sit up.

So, I thought, I'm going to try to stand up. And I went down. I couldn't stay up because I was losing feeling in my left leg, and my equilibrium was gone. As I was trying to stand, I kept saying to myself, I'm not staying down. I'm not the kind of person to get knocked down and stay down. I am not staying down!"

He was adamant and defiant, as he tried to fight off the growing paralysis in his legs and arm.

So, by the fifth or sixth time he tried to get up, he had worked his way 15 feet into the bathroom, standing and falling down. Then he reached up and grabbed one of the handicap bars in the bathroom and tried to pull himself up. But his efforts were futile, so he gave up the fight.

"I was just standing up and falling, and I couldn't stay standing even holding the handicap bar. So, I fell on the floor for the last time and crawled out of the bathroom."

Exhausted, he lay motionless, listening to the chatter and noise of people working out, unaware that something serious had happened in another part of the gym.

At the first pencil break, Lloyd didn't realize what had happened. He just wondered why his body was no longer cooperating with his brain. Then, as he was trying to stand and couldn't, he realized what it really was, that there was nothing he could do about it, and that he would have to lie still, praying help would come soon.

Then he realized that, though the stroke seemed to have happened suddenly, it had begun when he was at the supermarket and was beginning to affect his speech. To him, his speech was normal, but the woman at the grocery store noticed he avoided conversation, which was unusual for Lloyd.

No one could detect that a blood vessel in his brain had a weak spot and was swelling to the point of bursting. But it didn't happen until he was at the gym, most likely from the stress of working out. After it happened and he was lying helpless on the floor, he began to think about where this was leading; where life would proceed from here; how to handle it if he remained paralyzed. And he began to pray. Not so much for himself, but for his family because, if this was the end for him, his family would carry a heavy burden for a long time.

"No matter what condition I'll be in," Loyd was thinking, "we have to accept it and turn it over to God because we trust Him. Only He can change things we can't do anything about."

In his case, with this kind of stroke, the cards were against survival. Sometimes, but rarely, people do recover. Sometimes they can be fixed with surgery depending on the type of stroke. But he would think about that later. For now, he was totally dependent on God, who may have intended it to happen, Lloyd thought. If so, Lloyd figured He had a good reason. As he thought about it, one of his favorite scriptures came to mind:

Whoever dwells in the shelter of the Most High will rest in the shadow of the Almighty. I will say of the Lord, "He is my refuge and my fortress, my God in whom I trust. Psalm 91:1-2

Scanning the room, as he always did for safety reasons when people were exercising at the gym, one of the workers noticed a body a distance away lying on the floor motionless. Thinking the man had passed out or was injured, he hurried over to him, phone in hand.

"Man, are you okay?" he asked in a concerned voice.

"No. I think I'm having a stroke," Lloyd said, trying to stay calm. "Would you please call 911 for me?"

No longer had he asked, one of the gym owners, who had been watching the monitors, was on her way to where Lloyd lay unable to move, knowing that with a stroke, time was of the essence. A hemorrhagic stroke, which is what she suspected, usually happens suddenly with severe symptoms that can worsen quickly. And the closest hospitals were at least 25 minutes in either direction from where Lloyd was lying.

She had known Lloyd for years since he began frequenting the gym. And now, she feared for his life as he lay helpless on the floor amid the hustle and bustle of people coming and going, noisy treadmills and conversations.

Kneeling beside him, she said calmly as she could, "Hello, Lloyd. I saw what was going on. I already called 911. So, the ambulance is on its way. Are you able to move your legs?"

"No."

Your arm?"

Lloyd's answers to her questions, as he struggled to move his uncooperative left side, his speech slightly slurred, were recognizably negative. There was nothing she could do for him except keep him warm and comfortable and stay with him until help arrived.

By this time, the room had grown quiet, their attention drawn to the person lying on the floor a short distance away. Sensing something was seriously wrong, people who were exercising stopped their activity, wondering what was going on. Soon, as they stood watching, they heard a siren outside the door and saw medics hurry into the room carrying a gurney. It was then that they recognized it was Lloyd. Most of them knew him because it was a small town, and they were concerned. But their questions would have to wait.

Lloyd's youngest daughter Katie, who knew nothing about what was happening, was on her way to her home in Becker when something told her to take a different route than her usual shortcut. Not realizing why, nor thinking it unusual, she passed the street that would take her home and followed the route that passed the gym instead.

As she approached the parking lot, she saw her father's vehicle there and an ambulance with back doors open parked in front of the gym. Curious about who the patient might be, she quickly parked the car and hurried into the gym, wondering if something had happened to her father. After entering, she saw a man lying on the floor unconscious, surrounded by medics who were finishing hooking him to monitors in readiness for transport.

"Can I be of help here," she asked the medic, as she approached the man lying on the floor. She knelt down and touched his bare arm. "His skin is pretty cool and clammy, both signs of stroke," she said. "I'm a nurse, and that's my father. I was on my way home when I saw the ambulance out front."

While waiting for the medics to get Lloyd into the ambulance, Katie drove a few blocks away to get her mother, who was unaware of her husband's stroke, and asked if she needed a ride to the hospital.

"No, I'll drive myself," her mother responded," and hurried to get into her vehicle.

In the meantime, Katie called her sister, Brianna, who was at work. "I'll pick you up in a few minutes," she said urgently. "The ambulance is about ready to leave." Then she returned to the patient the medics were lifting into the ambulance.

"He hasn't been diagnosed yet, but we're treating him as a stroke victim," one of the medics told her. "We'll try to get to the hospital as fast as we can." Then, looking at Katie, who appeared troubled, he said, "Don't worry, we always watch the road carefully. We'll meet you at the emergency room."

He was about to close the ambulance doors when Katie stopped him. "Can my mother ride with him?" she asked, indicating her mother who was waiting in her car with the engine running.

"No." one of the medics replied, as he climbed in the vehicle. "We need to hurry. If you want, you can follow."

"I have to pick up my sister," Katie told him. "Shouldn't take long. I'll catch up and meet you there."

Without saying more, the medic quickly drove off, sirens blaring, lights flashing warnings for other drivers to clear the road, as the vehicle carefully turned onto the highway carrying precious cargo in their charge.

"I'm not waiting for you to pick up Brianna," Vicki called back to her daughter, and began to drive off, hoping she could catch up with the ambulance.

"Ok. We'll be there soon." Katie yelled, and hurried off to pick up her sister.

As Vicki drove, she tried to calm herself, praying urgently for Lloyd's recovery until she reached the hospital, all the way knowing her husband was in God's hands and could take him at any moment if that was His will. And that there wasn't anything she or her daughters could do about it. It was like a nightmare unfolding in front of her, and she wanted it to go away.

"This can't be happening," she thought, as she approached the hospital. That it had happened, and so suddenly, was beyond what she or anyone else could comprehend. "Maybe it's not as bad as we think it is," she said to herself, trying to be positive.

Though she wished what was happening wasn't real, she knew it was and would have to deal with it. Lloyd was his usual self when he left for home that morning, the sun brightening everyone's spirits. And now, it seemed, his life was hanging like a straw in the wind leaving his family to wonder if he would survive.

3

THE HOSPITAL

*I cried out to God for help; I cried out to God to hear
me. When I was in distress, I sought the Lord.*

PSALM 77:1-2.

The ambulance slowed as it pulled up to the emergency room
where the medics quickly opened its back door, brought him
out, and delivered him to the nurses, who were anticipating his
arrival. Lloyd was then taken to one of the trauma bays where
the nurses assessed his condition, hooked him up to monitors
and fluids and readied him for a routine Cat Scan to confirm the
prognosis.

After the scan was finished, he was placed on a gurney and
covered with a blanket. The nurse, who was in the imaging room
was about to take Lloyd back to the emergency room when she
hesitated as though listening to something. The doctor looked at
her questioningly and asked if something was wrong.

"Did you hear that?" she asked.

"Hear what?" the doctor responded.

"Lloyd was talking."

"Oh? What did he say?"

"It was something about God and how He'll take care of you. I didn't understand the rest. Didn't you hear him?"

"No. But I don't think he knows what he's saying. Normally, people who are unconscious don't realize they're even talking."

"So, if he could talk and quote scripture, that means his brain on the left side wasn't affected?" the nurse asked.

"Only time will tell," the doctor said, as though he wasn't sure that was the right answer.

Satisfied with the doctor's explanation, the nurse wheeled Lloyd back to the emergency room, where he complained of being nauseous. Minutes later, the doctor hurried in to see how Lloyd was doing and explain the scan results to the anxiously waiting family. Before he could get the report on the computer screen, the nurse walked up to the doctor and told him about Lloyd's nausea.

"Should we medicate him for this?" she asked.

"We'll wait a while for that," the doctor explained. "Normally stroke patients don't come out very well if we have to intubate after taking the medication. He may come out of it on his own and won't need intubating. So, we'll have to wait a bit, keep a close watch on him, and see if things change."

With that, the nurse left the room so the family and the patient could be alone with the doctor, who sat down on a stool close to the computer screen and motioned the family to join him. Without hesitation, he told them bluntly what was going on in Lloyd's head.

"Your husband has suffered a hemorrhagic stroke with massive bleeding, which is extremely serious," he told Vicki and the girls, pointing to the affected area of the brain. "As a result, he's paralyzed on his whole left side, which means he can't do anything for himself."

Katie looked at her mother and sister, who appeared to be lost in the conversation, wondering what it all meant.

"The scans were pretty rough," Katie explained to them after the doctor was called out of the room momentarily. "The bleeding was in the main branch that goes into the central part of the brain, and it seemed to spill over into the rest of the brain as well. It looked like a big old butterfly."

When Katie told Vicki and Brianna about the bleeding, they became emotional. They were eager, yet somewhat fearful, to know what to expect given the doctor and Katie's explanation; whether he'll be that way the rest of his life, if the paralysis will eventually go away, or will he even live.

Minutes later, the doctor returned to the room and, anticipating their questions, explained carefully and as understanding as he could, what was happening and the possibilities for Lloyd's future.

"You probably know from looking at the scan there's nothing we can do to stop the bleeding," he began, directing his comment to Katie, knowing she was a nurse and would understand. "And, as long as it's bleeding, the worse his condition will get. In some stroke cases, we can do surgery. But in his case, it's not possible because there's more than one bleed, which makes it too dangerous."

The doctor stopped to see if Vicki and Brianna were understanding what he was saying. They seemed attentive but still overwhelmed and had no questions, so he continued.

"A hemorrhagic stroke can last as long as there is pressure on the brain, which can increase the paralysis. It can also cause loss of consciousness and neurological dysfunction. That's why it's crucial for the patient's survival to get the bleeding stopped as quickly as possible. But, in his case, there isn't much we can do to stop the bleeding." He explained.

"I'll be blunt with you. Very few people recover from this type of stroke, and without treatment, these strokes are almost always deadly. According to medical reports, survival rates for a hemorrhagic stroke are lower for patients older than 70, which being he is 73, puts him in that category."

It wasn't what the family had hoped to hear or prayed for. But in spite of the doctor's report, they kept praying, clinging to the hope that recovery was possible. Now they were afraid to ask the question the doctor knew would come next, the question most doctors dreaded answering because they knew from experience the heartbreak it would cause.

It was a question the doctor anticipated and was prepared to answer. He shut down the computer and glanced at the patient lying unconscious and helpless on the hospital bed. "There is a three-to-four-hour window after a stroke like this to determine whether he'll get better or even survive. There are three large bleeds on the left side of his brain. Even though he was talking and making sense, lots of times patients like this don't survive a hemorrhagic stroke. And the longer it bleeds, the worse the outcome."

Hearing no response, he said, "I'm sorry," and left the room.

After letting the doctor's words sink in, Vicki and the girls turned to prayer saying tearfully, "Okay, God, whatever you want to do. We know you can perform miracles, and you know how we feel. But it's up to you. We trust in you and place him in your hands."

Later, she told a friend, "I had a feeling he was going to survive. But we were just overwhelmed at all the waiting."

It seemed a week had gone by in one day, and they were still dealing with uncertainties. Though it was difficult for the family, they knew they had to be patient because that's what God expected from them.

After three or four hours had gone by, the doctor stabilized Lloyd and sent him in for another scan, after which he told the family, "Well, the good news is that the scans showed there were no changes."

"And that was a relief at the time," Vicki told her friend. "Now, with that news, Brianna and Katie and I thought we might be able to get through this. But then, again, the doctor said the next 24 to 72 hours would be critical."

Before the doctor left the room, he told Lloyd's family they needed to be prepared. He stopped momentarily and looked at them to make sure they were listening before saying, "That depending whether his condition remains or advances to the negative, you have to make a decision about letting him go. At this point, it could go either way. But the bad side of that is, if he stays stable for three or four days and he does progress, the road to recovery will be very long and require a lot of time and patience."

Vicki and the girls seemed at a loss for words. So the doctor paused again to make sure they understood what he was saying. "I know what you're going through, and I know you've heard this before. But, as a doctor, I've dealt with this kind of thing many times. It's part of my job. And believe me, it's never easy to give a family this kind of news. I'm very sorry."

The doctor searched their faces for responses to what he had just told them, wondering if they had questions that needed answers before he left the room again. But all he saw was dark silence as they tried to process all that had happened since Lloyd left for the gym that afternoon.

"I have to leave you now," he said, as he approached the door. "But I'll be back in a while. In the meantime, please discuss this among yourselves and decide what you think would be best for him."

Sensing the family's need of more time alone to process the heavy load he had placed on them, his doubts about Lloyd's recovery, and his words about the possibility of having to let Lloyd go, the doctor excused himself, knowing he was leaving a trail of broken hearts behind him. He knew they had been through a lot in a short time; more than most people could handle, and he could sympathize with them.

He turned and faced the door, his hand ready to open it when he stopped, looked at them for a moment as though wondering if he should say what he was thinking and finally said comfortingly, "What I can do is pray with you if you would like."

Vicki and the girls were surprised at what at the doctor had just said, because most doctors wouldn't have said it. And, at the same time, they were pleased to discover he was a Christian who loved the Lord. It meant he was a doctor they could identify with and trust because they all shared the same faith and could be open about it.

"Yes. We would like that," she said, speaking for all of them. "Let's do it."

The doctor shut the door against the chaos of hallway traffic and drew closer to the family as they gathered around him, then led them in prayer for Lloyd's recovery and comforting for his family.

When they were finished, the doctor explained that Lloyd had to stay medicated for a while to lessen the pain in his head. "I'll check in with you later," he said kindly, then walked out of the room, gently closing the door behind him, leaving the family speechless.

It was a lot for all of them to process, and the doctor realized that. Everything was moving faster than even he could comprehend, and the family, who was left with the final decision, didn't know what to tell him. All they knew was that time was of the essence, and the decision laid heavy on their hearts.

Vicki spoke first as they all sat down, ready to listen, trying to hold back tears. "If he wasn't where he needed to be and was going through a lot of suffering, and it was his time to be with the Lord, and that was God's plan for him, maybe letting him go would be best," she told the girls, realizing it would be heartbreaking for all of them.

"Maybe the doctor was right. Maybe I'm only thinking about myself when considering whether to let him go," she thought. But, the more she thought about it, she wondered if the doctor could be wrong because she had heard of cases where they said one thing about recovery, and the opposite had happened. But she also realized that sometimes things can suddenly turn the other way, whether good or bad, and doctors aren't to blame for that.

"The other thing to consider is what would Lloyd say if I were in his place?" Vicki told her daughters. "What if there's a chance that, with prayer and proper care, he could recover, and we gave up too soon?" She stopped and thought for a while, then said, "I'm for giving him the chance. What do you think?"

Katie and her sister considered her words, admitting they made sense, and then agreed, though they were still overwhelmed with all that had happened. Besides that, they hadn't had time to turn their premature grieving into hope that he would survive. It was too short to allow their brains to comprehend all of it, and the imperativeness of getting it right was the priority of their lives right now.

"Either we could see a miracle in the works or we could see something going terribly the other way," Vicki reasoned, as she spoke to a friend about Lloyd's condition. "And we weren't sure how we would walk through that. Imagine hearing this about Lloyd, and then that more than a few hours earlier he was at the gym working out and doing perfectly fine. It was all so sudden. Now we're all just fighting for Lloyd and trying to remain calm."

We wait in hope for the LORD; He is our help and our shield. In Him our hearts rejoice, for we trust in His holy name. Psalm 33:20-21.

When the doctor returned to talk to them about their decision, he just listened, then said, "Okay." perhaps thinking he had said enough and praying they were right. "I'll schedule another scan to see if there's been any change. It'll take a while, but while we're waiting, we'll all hope and pray for the best."

Vicki and the girls nodded their approval, after which the doctor disappeared again into the sounds of visitors coming and going and doctors and nurses making their rounds.

The doctor continued Lloyd's care as though he were bound for recovery, possibly thinking that soon the family might have to face the fact that he wasn't going to make it because, unless there was a miracle, his chances were almost nil. But it was their decision, and he would do everything he could to make him well. Now the family would have to wait until the second scan and hope it wasn't too late.

Waiting in a quiet hospital room with no conversation between them, their individual thoughts about what had happened since they all got up that morning, and trying to put the pieces of a broken day together, were playing on their emotions.

"Through it all, Mom was very emotional, and so was Brianna," said Katie, who was only calm one. "As for me? I was very calm and matter of fact that this was happening. Just thinking we would have to deal the best we could with whatever was to come and that somebody's got to be calm in the midst of chaos. And then, Dad said Jesus was in the corner of the room, and I started to panic a little bit."

4

JESUS IN THE ROOM

As for God, His way is perfect; the Word of the Lord is proven; He is a shield to all who trust in Him.

PSALM 18, 30.

Jesus stood in a corner of the hospital room, big as life, unseen by others who were in the room with Him but clearly visible to the patient who lay quietly in bed, eyes closed. Lloyd could feel the love and compassion reflected in Jesus' face as He stood quietly waiting for Lloyd to acknowledge Him.

"Take a look over there," Lloyd told the small group that had gathered near his bed. "He's standing right there," he said, indicating the corner of the room where he saw Jesus standing.

"Who?" Vicki asked.

"Can't you see Him?" At his request, they turned around and looked, and seeing no one, they denied that anyone was there.

When the patient audibly mumbled something about Jesus' presence, his family, while standing at his bedside, began searching for signs of life, watching his chest rise and fall. And, as they anxiously waited for signs of recovery, they immediately went into panic mode expecting his last breath and the room monitors to straight line. What his family hadn't understood was that Lloyd was still alive under the influence of medication, conversing with his best friend.

Alarmed at what her father had said, Brianna, who was in tears, picked up her phone, called the pastor and told him what Lloyd had said about seeing Jesus in the room and that they thought it meant he was about to pass on.

"He's just medicated and doesn't realize what he's saying," said the nurse who was with them. "He's okay."

Then Brianna and Vicki, ignoring what the nurse had just said, hovered over Lloyd's bed, hugging him and praying for him.

"And I just stood there, taking it in," Katie said. "Then, his nausea went away, so the doctor said they probably wouldn't have to intubate. It just depended on what the MRI revealed."

Lloyd, who was still unconscious and unaware of what was going on around him, was listening to what Jesus was saying as He continued to stand in the corner of the room.

"Lloyd, if you're listening," He said kindly, "I have a question for you, and it's very important that you think carefully before you answer."

"I'm listening," Lloyd answered politely.

"Would you like to come with me, or would you like to stay here with your family?" Jesus' words, though distant and kind, were clear to Lloyd, but he wasn't sure what they meant. Perhaps because he didn't know he had a choice.

"I didn't answer Him right away," Lloyd said, "because I thought it was a trick question. I knew what I wanted to say, but I was afraid of giving Him the wrong answer; the answer He didn't want or expect from me."

Jesus, of course, knew the answer before Lloyd voiced it, for nothing escapes Him. And Lloyd knew that. Lloyd also considered that going with Him might be a chance to avoid the worries of a world that was headed in the wrong direction and exchange it for a peaceful, loving existence with his God, who would give him a perfect body.

"Who wouldn't want that?" he thought. "Jesus would understand." Lloyd thought a little longer. "No, that would be too easy, perhaps even selfish after all that Jesus went through."

Perhaps Lloyd was also thinking going with Jesus would leave a huge burden on the family who would be trudging on in an imperfect world without his help and advice. He remembered what he had once told them and hoped they would always remember it too.

"Yes, we'll go through some tribulation, and this country of ours is going to go back to the way it was supposed to be. It will take a lot of work; it will take a lot of standing up fighting and on our knees in prayer and just being stubborn about not giving in. And we must keep doing it over and over again."

He also remembered how good God had been to him and his family, and Lloyd wanted to make people aware of who He is, his power, his love, and His presence in their lives, even when they carry heavy burdens they can't handle alone. They needed to know these things before it was too late. Perhaps that was God's purpose for him because He knew Lloyd could handle it.

While this was going on in Lloyd's head, his family, heads bowed in tearful prayer, was pleading for his recovery, perhaps telling God it was important that he remain as head of a family, all of whom needed him.

Finally, thinking of the impact on his family and church if he should go, and the witnessing he could do to glorify the Father if he didn't go, Lloyd told Jesus in a soft voice, "I want to stay down here." Immediately after his answer was spoken, he thought he may have given Jesus the wrong answer. But his worry was short lived.

"Right after I had made my choice, there was a voice in the distance, and I heard Jesus say, 'God is pleased with your decision. I understand your suffering. It won't be easy for you, but you needn't worry. I will be at your side every minute of every day and night.' Relieved, I relaxed all over, inside and out at His response, and I considered that what I was going through was a blessing."

Lloyd considered it a blessing because perhaps, through his witnessing to people about his stroke and God's miracles, he could teach others about the grace of God and what He could do in their lives if they would let Him.

Then Lloyd got to thinking about who Jesus was when he came to Earth long ago, a man who was loved by some, hated by others, and would suffer tribulations far worse than anything Lloyd or anyone else would go through. And, like Jesus, Lloyd didn't have a choice.

5

ABOUT JESUS

And the Word became flesh and dwelt among us, and we have seen His glory, glory as the only Son from the father, full of grace and truth.
JOHN 1:14.

Jesus was the man who once walked the streets of Galilee, a man some people hated and others loved and were drawn to Him. He was a man who healed the sick, the blind, and the lame. A man who asked 12 men to put their trust in Him, leave their work, their homes, money, and everything they owned to follow Him.

Jesus was the man whose heavenly Father, though He loved his only Son, and it grieved Him to do it, gave Him into the hands of evil men. He knew it would cause His Son great suffering and death. But it was the only way people could reconcile themselves to Him and be saved from Satan's clutches. He was the sacrificial lamb, perfect in every way.

Jesus understood human grief, because he, also, suffered grief when He walked on earth. He wept when hearing of John the Baptist's brutal death at the hands of an evil king. *Matthew 14:9-12.* And He wept when, in the Garden of Gethsemane, He asked his Father if what was about to happen could be avoided, providing it was His Father's will; because He knew how brutal it was going to be. *Matthew 26:37-39.*

Jesus was the man who was victorious over death and rose from the dead that those who repented, even after committing the vilest crimes and believed in Him, would be forgiven for their sins and spend eternity with Him in heaven.

As Satan suggested, Jesus could have chosen not to obey His Father or to use His power to escape what was to come. But He didn't because he needed to be an example for humans regarding obedience. He could comfort them when they were suffering at the hands of evil, grieving at the loss of a loved one, fighting illness or otherwise, and could help them through it because He had experienced suffering himself. This is the man who with his Father and the holy spirit shows everlasting and unconditional love for His people.

In those times of silence with no activity in his room, Lloyd pictured from scripture everything the soldiers did to Jesus, all out of inexcusable and selfish hate: the soldiers who, while mocking Him, spat on Him, and proudly placed a crown of thorns on His head, twisting it into his flesh until the blood ran down His face; the soldiers laughing and mocking Him while flogging Him, and beating Him nearly to death.

By this time, Jesus was so weak, he could hardly stand up. But, in obedience to His Father, He said nothing, nor did He cry out because He loved people and wanted to bring all of them to the Father. When they reached Golgotha, the place where thieves and other criminals were to put to death, the soldiers forced Jesus to carry the heavy wooden cross that would finish taking His life, laughing and mocking Him while He stumbled and fell under its weight, the weight being the sins of all mankind.

Jesus never complained as soldiers stretched Him out on the

cross, and with pleasure and strength, pounded long nails into His hands, feet and wood, then raised the cross for all to see.

"Here is your king of the Jews," the soldiers proudly yelled to the crowd that had gathered there, and as though proud of their handiwork.

While on the cross in unbearable pain, close to breathing his last, Jesus cried out to His Father, thinking He had forsaken Him, but at the same time, knowing it was the only way to save mankind from Satan and that His father had ordained it. Just before he took His last breath: *"Jesus cried out in a loud voice, Father, into your hands I commit my spirit." Luke 23;46.*

Though Jesus died on the cross, it wasn't the end, because, if He hadn't risen from the dead, Satan would have had his way and death would have been permanent.

Who killed Jesus? It wasn't the soldiers who nailed Him to the cross. It wasn't the soldiers who pierced His side. It wasn't the people who yelled "Crucify Him! Crucify Him!" or those who chose Jesus to be nailed to the cross while an evil criminal was freed to commit crimes again. It was sins of the world that Jesus carried to the cross that if we would believe in Him and choose to follow Him, we would be forgiven.

It was a lesson the man on the cross next to Jesus quickly learned as he said, *"Jesus, remember me when you come into your kingdom." And Jesus answered him, "Truly I tell you, today you will be with me in paradise." Luke: 42-43.*

Believing was the only way. Lloyd would never forget it, and he wanted others to know it as well.

Dr. David Jeremiah in the Jeremiah Study Bible NIV says this:

Jesus, the risen Christ, is the man who appeared unknown to his disciples while walking to Emmaus. The story of the disciples on the Road to Emmaus is important for many reasons. It provides an emphasis on the Old Testament prophecies related to Jesus, evidence regarding an additional appearance of Jesus, and a connection regarding the many eyewitnesses of the resurrection as He opens our eyes, points us to the Word, and reveals Himself along life's walk as the resurrected Savior and Lord.

The story about the Road to Emmaus is only found in Luke 24:1-8; and 36-43 in the Jeremiah Study Bible.

6

THE VERDICT

O Lord of hosts, blessed is the man who trusts in You.
PSALM 12.

While all this was going on in everyone's heads, time clicked on slowly, never missing a beat, seeming to follow the rhythm of the patient's heart, while the family waited as patiently as they could for the doctor's MRI report. As the minutes passed, they kept glancing at the clock on the wall, anticipating the door opening, and hoping it would be any second. It was like waiting anxiously for a jury to walk into a courthouse room after a long, sometimes indecisive deliberation to deliver a verdict that would determine life or death for the defendant.

Some of them engaged in conversation while waiting. Others were deep in prayer. All of them expressed their fear that he might never come home again and wished for his survival. In a sense, Lloyd was a prisoner in his own body, unable to move, falsely accused, with no sign of release. The doctor was the jury, and the stroke the jailkeeper. The family sat together on hard courthouse benches, some of them pacing, all of them eager to hear the prisoner's fate because their lives depended on the verdict as well.

In the silence of waiting, all kinds of outcomes went through their heads. How would they take care of him if he did come home unless the paralysis would go away? But they knew the chance of that was beyond reach. Unless . . . But that would be a stretch. There was so much he couldn't do for himself. Walking, and using his left arm and hand were huge problems. They were problems that required miracles to fix, and only God could help with that. What they needed was faith and patience, both of which were difficult to hang onto at a time like this.

What seemed like hours later, the doctor pushed the door open, walked in, and closed it carefully, the expression on his face solemn, leaving the family to wonder what he was thinking. The family searched his face anxiously as he pulled a stool up to the computer and sat down, not wanting to hear the verdict but needing it to go on with their lives.

"Well, the results have come back," he said, as he stopped typing and faced them. "Sorry to keep you waiting. Would you like to see them?" Knowing what the answer would be, he motioned the family to gather around him. All of them were straining to see the images, some of them unable to determine what they meant, all of them eager for him to explain.

"At first, I was confused," the doctor admitted. "I was thinking these were someone else's scans because they showed that the bleeding had stopped. And I was thinking, this couldn't be. This usually doesn't happen with this kind of stroke. Maybe I got his report mixed up with someone else's. There must be some mistake. But then I checked it again and confirmed that these were definitely Lloyd's scans."

He looked over his shoulder at the faces that were still staring at the computer in misbelief, their expressions reflecting confusion. Then he went on. "It's still unbelievable because there is no reason this could have happened. We're told only one in four people who have had a hemorrhagic stroke will survive. They usually die within days or weeks after the stroke."

For a moment, Vicki and the girls looked at one another as though wondering if they should believe what the doctor was telling them. Especially since they were ready for the worst but praying for the best. Now there were expressions of amazement and relief on their faces, as they voiced thanks to God.

"Our prayers have been answered," the doctor agreed with a smile. "You can tell Lloyd about this when he comes around again. He's still unconscious for a little while."

"Does this mean he's going to recover from this?" Vicki asked hopefully. "And possibly get back to normal?"

"Getting back to normal will be up to him," the doctor said. "But don't expect it to be anytime soon; these things take time and a lot of physical therapy. And with it he will go through pain and frustration. Many patients get discouraged because they're not progressing fast enough and want to give up. So, he'll need as much support as he can get from family and friends. Don't let him even think of quitting because, with God's help, I'd say he can make it."

"We won't let him quit. You can be assured of that," Vicki said adamantly, her spirits rising. "We'll be right there for him when he needs us. And we'll keep praying for him. Thank you for everything."

"Don't thank me. This was all God's doing. He's the one who needs thanks," the doctor said. "And Lloyd is the one who has to do the work. The first thing is to get him conscious again. Then, when he's up to it, we can start therapy. He'll begin in the hospital. It will be slow at first. Then, after a while, as he advances, he'll be transferred to another location to continue. I'll keep you informed."

Lloyd's family again expressed their gratitude to the doctor, who was leaving the room so they could process what he had said. Then they gathered in prayer to thank God for the miracle that had taken place in Lloyd's body so far and asked for blessings and further healing during his physical therapy.

When the doctor left the room, Vicki picked up her phone and called the pastor to update him on Lloyd's condition. "Please keep him on the prayer chain. We're grateful for everyone who prays for him."

"That's wonderful news," the pastor said. "I knew they couldn't keep Lloyd down very long. I'll pass this on to the prayer chain right away and thank God for the work He's done and continues to do in Lloyd's body."

"Thank you. I'll let you know when he's able to have visitors," Vicky told him. "I know he'd like that. And, besides, having people around him is a necessary part of the healing process."

"We just went from there, day by day watching for progress," said Katie, who often visited him when he was in the hospital and in rehab. "The main thing was that my dad was struggling with migraines and, with the hemorrhagic stroke, we had to keep his blood pressure down. Every day was kind of routine. We were checking sensations and strength in his arms and legs for improvement and testing his memory as well.

It seemed the stroke hadn't affected his brain too much because he always remembered his name and where he was," Katie said. "But he was very sleepy. And the medications contributed to that."

7

THE JESUS MAN

I will praise you, Lord, with all my heart; before the "Gods" I will sing your praises. I will bow down toward your holy temple and will praise your name for your unfailing love and your faithfulness.

PSALM 1;38.

As the days went by, Lloyd lay on his hospital bed very much alive, and after his mind was clear, the doctor told him everything that had happened because he had no knowledge of what went on around him, what he had said or to whom he had said it. Because Lloyd had been sleepy most of the time, there wasn't much he did remember.

One morning when the doctor entered Lloyd's room, the shades were down, shutting out the sunshine, and he thought Lloyd was sleeping. As he glanced toward the bed, he was sure he heard someone talking. But there was no one else in the room except the patient. Because he knew people in an unconscious or confused state often talked, the doctor walked up to where Lloyd was lying with his eyes shut and heard him softly speaking.

"Blessed is the man who trusts in You." He was also repeating, "Through the blood of Christ, we can do this."

When Lloyd showed signs of awakening, the doctor walked to the window and lifted the shade part way to allow some light into the room, at the same time remembering his eyes were sensitive due to the stroke. "You've been talking," he said. "Were you aware of that?"

"Was I?" Lloyd asked. "What was I saying?"

"Yes, you were. This isn't the only time you've been talking in your sleep. And I wasn't the only one who heard you. We had to keep you sedated for a while because you were having severe headaches. It was the medications that made you unconscious or confused and unable to remember talking. You're not the only one who responds to a stroke this way."

Lloyd, who had been a born-again Christian for many years, was surprised to learn he had been talking, and wondered if he had said something he shouldn't. Something that would be offensive to God and others.

"I need to be a good example," Lloyd told him. "So, it wouldn't be good if I had said something God didn't approve of."

"No." the doctor was quick to say. "You didn't say anything bad. You were witnessing to everyone who would listen, about the greatness of the God you worship and quoting scripture. I'm told you were even witnessing to the medics on the way to the hospital and the nurses and doctors when you arrived. And that's what they've been telling me."

Lloyd was about to interrupt him when the doctor continued. "I've heard many people, who were unconscious or sleeping, unknowingly talk about various things, some of them not so nice, but never quoting scripture.

It's particularly amazing that you can remember scripture and even that you can talk so well, because, and you may have been told this, the left side of the brain handles speech and communication. Often times a stroke will wipe out parts of a person's memory and speech depending on how extensive the bleed is. And the bleed in your head was pretty extensive."

"I wasn't aware of that," Lloyd said. "I'm thankful the stroke didn't wipe out my speech because I have much to tell people. I'm also thankful I didn't say anything I would have regretted."

"I have to leave now," the doctor said. "But, before I go, I have to tell you, one of the nurses who took care of you told me she was a member of your church and remembered exactly what you were saying while under medication." He paused momentarily, then said, "Let's see. Her name is Christie. You should talk with her when you get a chance. She has a lot to tell you."

"I know who she is," Lloyd said. Then wondering what he meant about her having a lot to tell him, he quickly added, "I'll talk to her the next time I see her."

That afternoon when his wife visited him, Lloyd asked if she had heard him talking while his mind was unclear. "You were saying all sorts of things. Some of them didn't make much sense, like telling everyone you saw Jesus in the room."

"I don't even remember being put in the ambulance. And I didn't remember when someone told me about seeing Jesus in the room. I don't remember any of it," Lloyd told her.

"Well, you were pretty sedated and didn't know what you were saying," she said.

A few days later, Christie walked into Lloyd's room. "I don't know if you remember me. I'm Christie. I hear you want to talk to me."

"Yes. I remember you," Lloyd said. "You go to our church."

"I wouldn't blame you if you didn't remember me because I miss church a lot," she said. "I often have to work on Sunday. But I do remember you."

Lloyd was about to say something when she reached for the blood pressure cuff and said, "I'll check your blood pressure first, and then I can answer your questions." When she was finished, she sat down by his bed and began telling him what he had said while unconscious.

"It's true, what you said about Jesus being in the room with you," she said. "Not only did you see Him, you were talking to Him; something about staying here, and I didn't catch the rest. Like others in the room at that time, I didn't see Him either. But I believed you. And when you told people Jesus was in the room, and your wife insisted no one else was there, you said, 'take a good look. He's there.' And you were pretty adamant about it."

Lloyd looked at her and shook his head. "I don't remember any of that."

"The other thing is, when I first came into your room after you regained consciousness, as I walked in the door, the Lord told me He would draw you to me in a powerful way to be the one to take care of you. And I couldn't believe all of what I was hearing about you."

Lloyd looked at her as though puzzled. "What were you hearing about me?"

"You know; all the witnessing. You were quoting scripture, talking about Jesus and about how He died for us. Let me see. One scripture I remember was *Blessed is the man whose strength is in the Lord*. I remember that because your testimonies made a big impression on all of us, because we knew what your condition was. And you never gave up.

I have a lot more to tell you," Christie said. "But I don't have time right now. I'll write some of it down when I get time to think. But, because of my schedule, it'll be a while before I can get back to you."

Lloyd looked at her as though disappointed as he said, "Thank you for coming. I'll look forward to your next visit."

Christie smiled in assurance. "Don't worry. I won't forget."

With that, she left the room leaving Lloyd to think about what she had told him. Now, he felt a little better about what he had been saying and would no longer concern himself about those moments of unconsciousness or confusion, he thought to himself.

"From what the doctor told me about what Christie was saying regarding my witnessing," Lloyd told some of his visitors, "The only thing I could say is the Holy Spirit was working in me in a very strong way. And it was the Holy Spirit that told Christie to take care of me."

Though they may not have said it to Lloyd, many of the nurses, doctors, and others who heard his witnessing, wondered how anyone going through medical problems like strokes that threatened their lives or changed them drastically, could be thankful for it. No one they knew of would joyfully go through something as serious as Lloyd was going through with such a positive attitude and trust in God when many people would have cursed Him for it. To them it was like a person who was hit by a car, crippled for life, and thankful for his or her life being ruined.

For Lloyd, the stroke was a blessing because he was still alive when others in the same situation would have passed on or, if they had lived through it were crippled for life and blamed God because it happened. Those were the people who needed Him most; the ones who needed Lloyd's witnessing. To Lloyd, it was a blessing because God chose him to witness in His behalf for the miraculous healing taking place in his body. And that He could do the same for others who had faith in Him.

When he told his family about the stroke being a blessing, at first, they thought, not only had it affected his body, it had affected his mind in a very strange way. And they told him that because they didn't understand. So, he explained that it was the Holy Spirit speaking through him during his stay at the hospital.

One day, a different nurse came into his room, and told him she heard about his witnessing. "You said that in God's good grace and mercy, He spoke to you with the power of the Holy Spirit. It was about what Jesus can do in a person's life. You also quoted John 3:16 where Jesus said whosoever believed in Him would have everlasting life."

"I said all that?" Lloyd asked. "Was there anything else?"

"You never said anything bad. It was all about scripture and Jesus." she said. "You were even witnessing to the cleaning lady. And she was surprised at what you had said, because all she usually hears is a lot of complaining."

The nurse paused, as though she had nothing else to say and began walking toward the door. As she was leaving the room, she added, "Like one of the other nurses said, we were all overwhelmed by this."

Lloyd was pleased with what the nurse told him because it meant that unbelievers were coming closer to becoming believers because of what they were hearing. And that believers were becoming strengthened in the Word of God.

A couple of weeks had gone by when, one afternoon after the hallways were quiet, Christie tapped on Lloyd's door. Hearing a faint "come in," she went in holding some papers in her hand.

"Were you napping?" she asked.

"No. Just contemplating. Come sit down."

"I have some information for you. Is this a good time to listen?"

"Of course," he answered. "I'm always eager to hear what you have to say."

"I wrote these things down because I didn't think I'd remember them," she said, as she pulled a chair beside his bed and began reading.

"As a Nura nurse, I see stroke patients nearly every shift," she said. "Some of them had symptoms that were resolved. But there were others whose symptoms had not been resolved. And, that left them and their families devastated and desperately seeking hope and healing.

Then every once in a while, there comes a patient who just touches our heartstrings in a special way. For me, it happened the first time I entered the room of a patient known in the unit as The Jesus Man. I received a report before going into the room that this patient was confused and able to move only on one side of his body and had a high fall risk."

She paused to look at Lloyd to see if he was listening. He had slight smile on his face, so she returned his smile and continued.

"He would try to get out of bed with a resistance that was hard to redirect. He needed risk restraint at times to prevent him from falling out of bed and needed help for all daily cares. The only thing more persistent than his attempt at getting out of bed, I learned, was his attempts to talk. Not just to answer orientation questions, but no, he wanted to talk about Jesus to everyone. This, I am certain is how he became known as the Jesus Man."

She paused and looked up again to see Lloyd's reaction, but he said nothing; just looked at her as though eager to hear more.

"I entered his room one morning like any other morning ready to greet my patient and start my day, thinking 'I can tell Jesus this is going to be a great day.' Much to my surprise, as I entered my patient's room, I knew the face staring back at me. Oh, my goodness, my patient, the Jesus man. It was Lloyd. He didn't recognize me because of his short-term memory loss. It was almost as though I were a new face every time I entered the room that day.

Yet, one thing was consistently clear. Lloyd had not forgotten Jesus. In the midst of chaos and care, in confusion and all the uncertainties of what was to come, Lloyd always had one thing he wanted to hear. Scripture. I remember hearing things like 'Hide scripture in your heart. Memorize and store it up. Make it a habit. Reserve it for times when you will need it.'

It was clear to me he had stored scripture in his heart, and when his mind was confused, his heart was not. So, he may have forgotten me or the routine for the day. But he never forgot Jesus. And clearly Jesus had not forgotten him."

When Christie finished reading, she handed the papers to Lloyd. "Here. You can keep these. Later on, when you've recovered, you can use them to remind you of what you were going through. Sort of like a journal. In the meantime, I'll keep praying for you."

"I appreciate your taking time to do this, and your prayers," Lloyd said. "Thank you. What you wrote was nicely done. I'll give them to my wife when she comes in again. She'll keep them in a safe place for me."

After she left the room to continue her rounds, Lloyd thought about everything she said. "I was amazed at what she was telling me and, at first, I didn't know what to say," he told Vicki when she came to visit that afternoon.

To Lloyd, his stroke was an opportunity to glorify Jesus and bring understanding to His life on earth. And God chose him for that purpose. While alone in his hospital room and the halls were silent, Lloyd had a lot of time to think. Especially about his condition and what the future might bring both for him and his family. He wasn't worried because he knew he was in God's hands, and with Him he would get through it. He also remembered that Jesus said recovery wouldn't be easy and might not be complete. And, that whatever the outcome was at the end of his recovery, he had to accept it thankfully because he belonged to God, who had a purpose for the rest of Lloyd's life.

"The different things our God has taught me boosted my

faith," Lloyd explained to those who would listen. "It has boosted my praying and my reading the Word of God. The Bible says, in all things give thanks. *Thessalonians 5:18; In everything give thanks: for this is the will of God in Christ Jesus. Rejoice always, pray continually.*

Be courageous in your tribulation. When we follow what God's Word says, we win no matter what state we're in because the reward is eternal life in heaven.

Everything in the Bible that God has written for us to read and follow is for us to have an abundant life," he would tell people. "That abundant life is found in the shed blood of Jesus Christ. And when we accept that, and follow Christ, our lives turn around completely 180 degrees away from what we were before salvation. And that peace, that joy, cannot be replaced by anything."

Lloyd thought of all of this and wanted to remember it because he would tell his story about God's miracles to people who came into his room in hopes they would understand the healing power of God and the unconditional love Jesus has for them.

WHO IS THE HOLY SPIRIT?

The Holy Spirit is the third person of the trinity, the trinity being Father God, Son Jesus and Holy Spirit. Often described as "God in three Persons, blessed Trinity." Three persons in one is similar to a human being; a father, a son, and a doctor. Though they are one person, they each have a different function. Specifically, the Bible describes the Holy Spirit as the following:

> *Do you not know that your bodies are temples of the Holy Spirit, who is in you, whom you have received from God? You are not your own. Corinthians 1:19.*

The Christian who is indwelt by the Spirit is indwelt by God. The Holy Spirit possesses the attributes of deity: omniscience, meaning all-knowing, aware of past, present, and future; omnipresence, capable of being everywhere at the same time; omnipotence, all powerful; eternality, timeless existence.

He does works only God can do, such as creating, regenerating and sanctifying. He is equally associated with the other members of the Trinity. Moody Bible Commentary.

Here is some scripture on the Holy Spirit:

He is God, and believers are baptized in His Name: Matthew 28:19-20.

He has the power to protect believers so that nothing can steal their salvation: Ephesians 4:30.

He dwells within believers and transforms them into the temple of God: 1 Corinthians 6:19-20.

This is an example of the way the Holy Spirit sometimes works:

One early evening, a mother and her teenage daughter were driving home from shopping in a nearby city. Her daughter was driving and wasn't wearing a seatbelt. As they approached town, the girl turned onto a city street where she lost control of the vehicle and crashed into a street pole. Her mother, who wasn't hurt, immediately got out and hurried to her daughter, whose arms were wrapped around the pole. When the mother asked her daughter if she was hurt, her daughter responded, "Mom, there's a man standing there. He asked me if I wanted to go with him. Can I?" Her mother, not seeing anyone around, realized what her daughter meant and gave her permission.

8

BEGINNING THERAPY

Consider it pure joy, my brothers and sisters, whenever you face
trials of many kinds, because you know that the testing of your faith
produces (patience) and perseverance. Let perseverance finish its work
so that you may be mature and complete, not lacking anything.

JAMES 1:3

Lloyd figured he had been in the hospital for a week or so where, when he was ready, they transferred him to inhouse rehab. Lloyd wasn't happy with most of it because it wasn't what he had expected.

When rehab began, Lloyd's daughter Katie sat by him with a pen and tablet each time she visited. On it, she recorded his progress so she could tell him later everything that had happened and what he had said, because he couldn't remember all of it.

Much later, when his mind had cleared from the medications, he asked her about his beginning days of therapy while in the hospital because he was certain he could do better than what his therapists would allow. He was disappointed in them, and didn't hold back when letting them know about it. It was his body, he thought, and he should know better than the therapists what he was capable of doing.

"How did I behave?" he asked her one day during her visit, afraid his temper may have gotten away from him.

"Well, your hardest time was with speech therapy," she said.

"Why? What did I do?"

"You got super irritated with the therapists because they made you do a lot of writing. And with physical therapy, you got really mad at them because they wouldn't let you do what you wanted. And the things they were asking you to do, you couldn't do them."

Lloyd chuckled, as though pleased with what he was hearing because he had a reason to be angry. "What were those things?"

"You wanted to move from your bed to a chair by yourself, and you couldn't even sit up in bed by yourself yet," Katie explained. "So, while the therapists were working with you on the a, b, c's, you were wanting to do the x, y, z's. And you hadn't even graduated yet. So, you got really mad when they wouldn't let you do what you wanted to do."

"What else did I do?" Lloyd asked curiously.

"You were having a hard time with speech pathology because they wanted you to sit up, and you got bad headaches when you sat up," Katie continued. "And you couldn't eat or drink unless you were sitting up, either. It was like taking one, two, three steps when you wanted to take a hundred. So, you were battling with all that stuff."

"That's because I knew I could do better," Lloyd insisted. "But they wouldn't allow me to try to prove I could do them. At least they could let me try, and that's where I think they were wrong."

Thinking he couldn't be the only one who had argued with their therapists, he looked at her and said sarcastically, "I wonder how many patients cooperate with that stuff."

"Not many," Katie responded, then tried to explain to him

what the therapist already knew but hadn't told him. And that was, trying to make him understand that his brain was mistakenly telling him he could do it, but his body was telling him he couldn't; at least not yet. So, his body and brain were arguing with each other. And that often leads to frustration, anger, disappointment, and then wanting to quit.

Katie wasn't sure her explanation sank in, so she continued.

"What you needed was patience," she said carefully. "Some people who are going through these things hate being here and are eager to get back to normal so they can go home. And I can't blame them for that. I understand it's not much fun to lie helpless with nothing to do just waiting for the therapist or visitors to come in. I also get it that patients heal faster when they're home surrounded by family who love them rather than here with strangers."

"That's very true," Lloyd said. "Well, at least there are others who have the same problems with therapy. So, I guess I fit right in."

After thinking about it, he told Katie he expected ahead of time that he would argue with his therapists. "But, in spite of it, I can tell you with all confidence and faith that every day I thank my God for allowing this stroke to happen to me."

During the long process of physical therapy, Lloyd's frustrations seemed never ending because he couldn't get up on his own and couldn't walk. Nor could he use his left arm. He was a prisoner in chains that were holding him back, and no one had the key to release him. Every time he became frustrated, which was often, he took his frustrations to God. "And He took care of them," Lloyd said.

"After the stroke happened, I had to have help with everything. My left side was completely gone, so we started working physical therapy on that side. We worked on my left hand some, then my left leg some." After each day's struggle, he made a little progress. And each day, though it was small, he thanked God for it.

"This was all because of the grace of God," Lloyd said to anyone who asked how he was doing. "It was nothing I did; it wasn't anything anyone else did. It was completely the Lord God."

One day, with the therapist's help, Lloyd was sitting up in bed when the pastor's youngest daughter and a few of her basketball friends walked into his room. The therapist had placed a spoonful of Jello in Lloyd's unstable left hand, and was standing by his bed watching as he tried to move the spoon to his mouth without spilling or dropping it.

"It was extremely difficult for me," Lloyd said. "It was a painful effort, trying to get my arm to cooperate."

As they watched him struggle, and figuring he could use some help, the girls began urging him on, chanting, "You can do it! you can do it!" They kept repeating it louder and louder until finally, the spoon reached his mouth without spilling. And Lloyd sighed in relief.

"As they chanted, I kept going and kept going, and I finally made it," he said, as though he had just lifted a one-hundred-pound weight with one arm. When the spoon reached his mouth, the girls and the therapist began clapping, and Lloyd smiled victoriously.

As his therapist began working on Lloyd's legs, he had him lie down in bed and began massaging his feet and toes to bring back feeling. After several days of this, Lloyd wasn't happy with his therapist because he had already accomplished moving his toes. He had been bored for quite some time without complaining when, finally, he suggested the therapist move to something more challenging. But the therapist, who had heard this argument from many of his patients didn't comply because he knew what he was doing, and they didn't understand.

"These exercises are to strengthen your arms and legs so you can learn to walk. And you're not ready yet," the therapist tried to explain, but to no avail.

Lloyd was about to argue when the therapist decided to continue defending his decision not to move on. "If I have you on your feet right now, you would be at risk of falling. And, if that happened, I would probably lose my job."

Lloyd still disagreed. "The only way I'm going to get strong enough to walk is to walk," he said bluntly. "Not by lying in bed wiggling my toes."

Though the therapist knew Lloyd wasn't ready to be on his feet yet and didn't appreciate his comment, he said nothing and continued therapy without change until he knew Lloyd was physically ready to move on.

9

THERAPY AT SARTELL SUITES

May the Lord of Israel keep you safe from all harm; may
he grant your heart's desire and fulfill all your plans.

PSALM 20.

Several days later, the physical therapist came into Lloyd's room, and after he finished working on him, he told him they weren't able to continue his therapy at the hospital. "So, you'll be moved to Sartell Suites and they'll pick up from here."

To Lloyd, it came as a pleasant surprise, because he was eager to move forward, which, so far, wasn't happening. "Why am I going to Sartell?" he asked.

"We think you've progressed enough that you're ready for the next step," the therapist explained, as he got ready to leave the room. "But we don't have the equipment for advancing much further with you. Sartell does, and it's close by. So, you'll be transported tomorrow."

Before leaving the room, he asked Lloyd if he had any questions. Seeing he didn't, the therapist wished him the best in his recovery, then added, "I hope I don't see you back here again."

Smiling, Lloyd took that as a compliment and politely thanked him for his help.

"God bless you, and have a good day," Lloyd said, as the therapist left the room.

Lloyd was happy that maybe now he could advance more quickly with equipment that would allow him to do more than what he had been given in the past few weeks. It was a fresh start, and he was looking forward to the change. So, the next day, they transported him to Sartell Suites near St. Cloud. It was still within reach of his family and his church, and he thanked God for that.

Lloyd was in Sartell Suites for approximately a month. Soon after he arrived, he complained about having headaches. So, they medicated him. That took care of the headaches, but caused other problems.

"After they gave me the medications, I saw a litter of kittens running around in the room. So, when I told the doctor this, he stopped the medications. After that, the cats stayed around in my head. But after a while, they disappeared."

Before the hallucinations had left entirely, they caused problems for Katie and the therapists, who reported that Lloyd had become combative and impossible to work with.

"As I lay in bed, they had to hold me down," he told Vicki the next time she visited. "I didn't know what was going on. And, because I was being restrained, I was frightened. The disappointment about that was that it only took one person to hold me down. I thought it would take three or four. But it was just one, so I accepted that," he teased.

When Lloyd had become combative, Katie was afraid he would have to remain restrained for a while. And she didn't want that to happen because she thought he would only become worse. To Lloyd, they were treating him like a naughty child who needed punishing. It was like the stroke that prevented him from functioning on his own.

"You were one-on-one for behaviors for a while because you were hallucinating," Katie explained to him when his brain had cleared enough that he could understand what she was saying and was acting like his normal self.

"What was I doing?" Lloyd asked her. "What do you mean one-on-one?"

"You were yelling at me and trying to get out of bed," Katie told him. "And, when I tried to stop you, you yelled, 'Get out of my way! I'm getting out of here!' And you tried to push me aside. Because you were a danger to yourself, a staff person had to be in your bedroom watching you at all times to prevent you from falling or being harmful to others. And I was trying hard to make sure you didn't need to be restrained, because I knew that would have been terrible."

Katie knew the hallucinations were the culprits causing her father's anger but that the medications were necessary to lessen the pain in his head. She also knew that, though he tried to push her aside, he wouldn't intentionally hurt her and figured he would have been disappointed with himself had he known how he behaved.

When Lloyd was at Sartell Suites, his headaches became less frequent, and his mind had cleared from the medication, the therapists decided he was ready to start therapy. So they decided to have him try walking in the hallway with a Hemi Walker. Unlike a regular walker, the Hemi keeps patients from falling while helping them gain strength in their legs. Each day, with the therapist's help, Lloyd kept a record of distance walked. And each day, he walked a little farther.

"One day, I said to myself that I was going to walk to the end of the hallway. So, I started walking. And when the therapist saw how far I had walked, he said, 'Wow. What's going on here? Aren't you tired?'"

Lloyd said "No. Not one bit. I'm going right to the end of the Hallway."

The therapist walked beside him to make sure he was okay. And when Lloyd got to the end of the hall, he stood the Hemi Walker next to himself, hit the wall with his right hand, and said, "I beat you today." Then he turned around and walked back to his room with the Hemi Walker. "It was a good day, because I had walked a little more than 300 feet both ways."

The Hemi Walker helped him gain strength and balance, he told people who didn't understand. "And it helped me have the tenacity to get up in the morning and get going."

Lloyd had been in Sartell Suites for a month, slowly making progress and seeing small miracles along the way when Vicki was told by their insurance company that their coverage was running out. And that meant Lloyd would soon have to be discharged or remain and pay Sartell Suites out of pocket, which would hurt them financially.

"Lloyd isn't finished with therapy yet," Vicki told them. "Healing isn't an overnight process; he still has a long way to go." Though she tried to make the insurance company understand, it seemed she was getting nowhere. How would they know what his situation was when they were sitting behind a desk all day, she thought.

"Our home isn't handicap equipped. There's no way I can get him down the steps at our home or even into our vehicle to get him there," she said. "Can't you give us an extension?"

Though Vicki asked, the insurance company wouldn't budge. They were adamant about the deadline to end coverage, and there wasn't anything they could do about it. They had a deadline, and they meant to keep it.

Frustrated with the insurance company, Vicki hung up and began making phone calls, trying to make someone understand the seriousness of their predicament. Reaching a dead end, she began the search for another place where the insurance company would allow them to continue his therapy. In her search, she found there were several places near their home, but they weren't taking additional patients.

Then she was told there was a place in Minneapolis that had room. But it was more than an hour away, and with rising gas prices, it would be too costly for back-and-forth travel.

"It was either going to be Shepherds of Grace, Sartell, or St. Bens," Vicki said. "You had to qualify for medical insurance through the state. And that meant I had to race around filling out paperwork. The last day before discharge, I called to verify if he had qualified through the state. And they said no, that his case hadn't been processed yet. I told them there was no way I could bring him home. But they had nothing to say about that."

Frustrated, and running out of options, Vicki called the director at St. Ben's and explained the situation. "I also contacted an elder care attorney and explained it to them. Then I called the insurance company back and told them, 'This is where it's at. I need an answer within the next three or four hours as to what you're going to do. Because, if you choose not to accept him or let him stay another 24 to 48 hours at Sartell, we'll have to pay out of pocket. That's the only option.'"

The clock kept moving forward as the nurses prepared Lloyd for transport, and Vicki was growing desperate not knowing what to do because every phone call was a dead end. She knew the amount of rehab he had already undergone wasn't enough. The insurance company should know that. And the longer they waited, the more difficult it would be to regain the progress he might lose in the waiting.

"So, we prayed hard that God would open a door."

Two and a half hours later, the insurance company called and told Vicki that medical assistance at Sartell would be provided. "Then we got a verbal okay for another 24 to 48 hours for the insurance, but we had to use Medicare as a supplemental and a backup. So that was something we were thankful for," she said. And, though it wasn't the best option because two days wouldn't be enough, she told the people at Sartell he would be staying.

In the meantime, God knew what was going on from the beginning and had a better solution. Lloyd and Viki both had faith that God wouldn't let them down, but as time was closing in on them and God hadn't revealed His plan yet, they were becoming anxious.

They were down to one hour before the Suites would have to release him or prepare him for staying, and the nurses weren't sure what it was going to be. Just when Vicki thought about God not letting them down, He gave her an option, and it was one phone call away. It was a different way they could get state insurance, and instead of sending him home or keeping him at the Suites, they would take him to St. Bens in a town close to home. And St. Bens was known for its good reputation.

Lloyd and Vicki knew how it played out was a miracle because all odds were against it happening so close to the deadline. They thanked God for it before they left, remembering He always said He would never forsake them, and He was right there beside them through it all. They also realized that when you ask God for help, He expects you to do some of the work, which Vicki had done. God helps those who help themselves and ask Him for help as well.

10

THERAPY AT ST. BENS

*Let the whole world bless our God and sing aloud his praises. Our
lives are in His hands and He keeps our feet from stumbling.*

PSALM 66.

When Lloyd arrived at St. Bens, the staff welcomed him, made him comfortable, and assured him and Vicki he would get good care while there. And they kept their promise. God had sent His guardian angels to watch over him day and night.

"This was a God-send because St. Bens is probably the best place in the area for me to be," Lloyd said when he heard where he was going. "And God most likely thought it best as well. Everyone was very cordial. They were really nice and professional. They knew what they were doing when they came into the room. They were there when I pushed the button for help, and were there when I walked with a Hemi Walker, which was a pretty heavy challenge for me."

Lloyd was pleased with the therapy at St. Bens because he could see advancement from one step to the next, and some of it was challenging. At the beginning, his equilibrium would sometimes be off, making it difficult for him to sit up in bed, stand up or walk.

"And they wanted me to stand still with nothing holding me," Lloyd said.

In those three or four weeks of practice standing still, Lloyd said he progressed from 30 seconds to 40 seconds to seven minutes. "There was one point when I was just preparing to get out of bed, waiting for the therapist to show up, and when he did, I sat up and felt no equilibrium problems. It was as though nothing had happened. No stroke. So, I thought, I'm going a step further and stand up. So, with the therapist watching, I stood up and had no balancing issues."

Another day, when his balance wasn't an issue, he stood up and thought he would walk to the window, three steps away, his therapist right next to him.

"I got to the window with perfect timing and with perfect balance. I looked outside and saw some people down at the courtyard. Then I walked a little, turned around, walked back to the bed, and sat down. It hadn't happened before, and it hasn't happened since. Although, I noticed improvements after I found it was easier to walk with a Hemi Walker. It's kind of vague how it happened, but it did happen. So that brought back memories of being able to walk again. And my equilibrium has improved from time to time."

When Lloyd first arrived at St. Bens, a young man, who was the type of person Lloyd asked God to provide for him, began his speech therapy, coming into his room once or twice a week.

"He's a believer," Lloyd told his visitors. "And when I told him what I thought about the stroke, he looked at me and said, 'You're absolutely right. I believe this has been a blessing for you. And it is.'"

JESUS IN THE ROOM

One Tuesday, the therapist walked in Lloyd's room, smiled, greeted him with a cheery hello as he usually did, and asked how he was doing. Lloyd, who was eager to have someone to talk with who shared his beliefs, cheerfully returned his greeting. That morning, he had much to talk about. And, he was pleased that now there was someone with whom he could comfortably share his love for Jesus.

"Some people don't understand what I've been through," Lloyd told him. "God walked me through it. There's nothing like the hand of God holding your right hand and walking you through something. It's the most calming, peaceful, joyful situation a person can be in."

"I think so too," the therapist said, as he began working on Lloyd's left leg.

Lloyd paused for a few seconds, then continued. "I had a friend who was in a lot of pain, and I'm praying he realizes this is a gift from God to bring him closer to Him. You know, a more in-depth relationship. So, no matter what anybody is going through, God is always there and will never leave us. His Word says so. It's His Word we have to depend on and take a look at daily."

"I agree. We need to stay in prayer," the therapist said. "We need to read His scriptures. The Bible says study to improve ourselves. And, if we love our Lord and want to know Him better, He'll be pleased with us."

As Lloyd continued talking, the therapist paused occasionally to listen, and then continued working.

"The different verses we run into, for instance," Lloyd said. "People ask me what my favorite verse is. And, I say, the verse I need to read is the time I read it."

The therapist nodded in agreement, catching what Lloyd was saying.

"But, at the same time," Lloyd said, "There's a verse in the

Bible that makes all this possible, a relationship with God, talking about Jesus, and doing everything the Bible says. And that has to be my favorite, John 3:16, because, without the blood of Jesus, we can't do it no matter what it is. We're completely dependent on the living God who created everything, who was always there for us and will always be there for us. His perfect plan for salvation is there for us to grab hold of even after we choose to follow Jesus and walk with Him and talk with Him."

While finishing his work, the therapist listened in amazement as Lloyd continued, because none of his other patients had talked to him about the Lord and what He could do in their lives. He was also amazed at how much he knew about the Bible, and asked him about it.

"I study it every day," Lloyd said. "And I memorize verses."

"Something that some people don't realize is that studying the Bible and being a believer doesn't make us perfect or special about doing it," Lloyd told him. "In fact, I'm just as special as anyone is. This stroke was a blessing and it still is."

After working with the speech therapist for a few weeks, Lloyd heard about a therapist named Maggie who worked with people who suffered brain damage and was considered an expert.

"My therapist wasn't there one day," Lloyd told a visitor. "So, I was handed over to her for one session."

Lloyd was immediately impressed with her abilities and knowledge regarding brain damage and decided he wanted her for his therapist. So, he prayed that, if it was God's will, He would make it happen. Having said that, the problem for Lloyd was how to kindly tell his present therapist he wanted to switch.

"How can I tell him without hurting his feelings?" he asked himself.

Lloyd needn't have been concerned because God has a way of taking care of things; and He did. The next time the therapist came into the room, Lloyd sat waiting in anticipation, knowing what he wanted to say, but not sure how to word it. He was ready to begin the conversation when the therapist took the lead. It was as though he knew what Lloyd was about to say. And perhaps he did.

"It's gotten to the point where I can't do much more for you because I don't have the expertise. So, if you don't mind, after today, I want to turn you over to Maggie. She's more versed in these kinds of strokes, and I think she'll do a better job for you."

Lloyd looked at him in surprise, because it wasn't what he expected. Because of what the therapist said, Lloyd wouldn't have to tell him about his conversation with God, which was a relief. And he thanked God that He had arranged it that way.

"I enjoyed having you as my therapist," Lloyd told him kindly before he left. "But I understand the circumstances. As you probably know, I knew about Maggie because she filled in for you in your absence last week. So, I don't mind the change."

Maggie was the therapist Lloyd had prayed about, not only because of her expertise, but also because he knew she was a Christian. "And I found out her husband is a believer also," he told a visitor with a smile. "I am so blessed to be surrounded by believing people with whom my wife and I can identify."

Then he added, "And unbelieving people who, through the power of the Holy Spirit, I can show what a Christian is – what Christ-following people mean to other people. That's what I live for.

Everything I've gone through and that God has walked me through has been a blessing," he would continue to tell people. "I have not once regretted the position I'm in right now. I have, as long as I remember, thanked God for my condition. I also thank God for my friends, my church family, and everything."

Though he thanked God for what he was going through, he

admitted that recovery was difficult, challenging and sometimes frustrating. But he had been advised of that when he gave his choice to Jesus. Sometimes he had tough days, especially dealing with migraines and frustrations about his progress. Even so, he reaches plateaus, and those are better days. But he never considers himself a victim.

"One day, I was talking to one of my therapists," he told Vicki. "And he started to say, 'You being a stroke victim . . .'" Hearing that, Lloyd quickly interrupted. "Just a minute. I'm not a stroke victim; I'm a stroke survivor. So, if any of you survived a stroke, God has you alive for a reason. He's not finished with you yet."

"That's a good way of looking at it," the therapist admitted. Then, without finishing his sentence, he encouraged Lloyd to continue.

"If you're ever down, look forward to what He's going to have you do. Worship God. Don't look down on yourself or anybody else that looks down on you. Feel sorry for them because they don't have the opportunity we have. Fellowship with our God to the power of the Holy Spirit. From the blood of Christ, we can do this. Stick with your therapy. Don't drop anything. God is going to protect you and work with you. He is going to bless you."

Lloyd paused, then went on to say, "After the stroke, when I figured out what was going on with me and God asked me if I wanted to go with Him or stay down here, I figured the stroke was a blessing."

Lloyd stopped talking for a minute, then told the therapist, "Someone I talked to asked me if I had it to do over again, would I. And I said yes, I would."

"I'm going to have to think about that for a while," the therapist interrupted. "I don't know of anyone who would say that, because most people don't survive a stroke like that; especially a second time. Have you ever considered the odds? If it should happen to you again, chances are better that you won't survive."

"Then I would still be a winner," Lloyd was quick to say. "Because I have faith in God. And I know where I'm going if I shouldn't survive."

11

THERAPY AT HOME

*Who is like you, oh Lord, among the gods? Who is like you,
glorious in holiness, fearful in praises, doing wonders?*
EXODUS 15:11.

Lloyd was doing inhouse therapy for two years, and then he was pronounced ready to be discharged to continue on his own at home and at the local gym. His legs weren't quite strong enough to walk on his own, but with therapy, he continued to do better. As he was reaching the end of his stay at St. Bens, the family worked on making their house and vehicle handicap accessible.

"I'm still doing therapy, of course," Lloyd told one of his church friends. "And I'm moving through it really well. I still have plateaus, but things are progressing, thanks to my therapist."

Lloyd always spoke well of his therapist, telling people, "She is absolutely top notch. It's her attitude, experience, and gifts in her chosen field. She's direct, up front and honest. And that's the way I like it. I can take criticism."

He also likes to tell his friends, "I'm still teachable in the ways of the Lord in what he is instructing me and teaching me to be.

The biggest thing that's real important to me is that I'm able to minister to people whether I'm on wheels or standing on two feet. I keep thinking maybe I'm able to minister to people better in a wheelchair than if I can stand up and walk without effort."

Lloyd frequently talks to his sister in Missouri who, from the beginning of his stroke, has kept track of his recovery. One day, when talking to her on the phone, she asked if he thought he would walk again, after which he told her how he felt about his stroke and recovery and the possibility of walking again.

"I want you to know, this stroke I've had and everything I've walked through because of it, has been a blessing for me," Lloyd told her. "And with Jesus, I'm at peace with where I am. Does that mean I don't want to walk again or drive again? No, it doesn't mean that either. What that does mean, is that I have open opportunities to share my faith with people."

"What kind of therapy are you getting right now," she asked.

"As you probably remember, I've been lifting weights since I was 12 years old," Lloyd continued. "So, I know exactly what I have to do when I go to therapy."

"Yes, I remember that," she said. "Go on."

"They let me use the leg press, starting with 30 pounds. But I only do one leg at a time. Because if you do both at the same time, you'll favor one leg. And the weak leg won't get the exercise it needs."

"That sounds logical," his sister said. "But I don't go to a gym. So, I don't know what a leg press is."

"I've heard it explained this way," Lloyd said.

"It's a machine used for a training exercise where a person pushes a weight or resistance away from them using their legs. It can also be used to evaluate an athlete's overall lower body strength and for rehab."

So, using the leg press, Lloyd told her, he has worked up to

80 pounds, and in a couple of weeks, he would work more with the left leg than the right leg.

Though Lloyd was pleased with his progress and decided to continue therapy, he sometimes thought his caregivers didn't agree and were trying to discourage him. "They kept telling me I've reached a level where I'm not going to get better. Most likely meaning I should accept that and move on. Although they didn't say it that way."

In spite of what they told him, Lloyd was adamant about keeping up with therapy, especially strengthening his legs that he might walk again. Not just a few steps, but across a room or farther by himself.

"The way it is right now, I do need help walking," he admitted to his sister. "But I expect that will change."

When his caretakers tell him further therapy won't help, Lloyd tells them, "I and other people have a God we have prayed to about my being able to walk and be totally healed. When I tell them that, the therapists tell me, "You're not going to be healed because, the part of your brain affected by the stroke is dead and can't be replaced. So, the good part of the brain has to make up for the part that was lost."

"What was your response to that?" his sister asked, because she knew he wouldn't believe what those people told him.

"I tell them, "You must not have the same God I've got. Because my God is going to heal this." Lloyd was insistent as he went on to explain. "When it happens, I want it to be seen by someone the Holy Spirit was working with to influence them to turn away from their sinful ways and follow Jesus. And that might be the key for them to do that. I don't want it (walking) right now. I want it to be at the right time."

Throughout his journey there were therapists who didn't understand and looked at Lloyd as though he were chasing a rainbow. But he knew better. Many people who think they're believers, find it difficult to give credit to God for good things that happen in their lives – things that couldn't have happened without God's intervention, and label them as coincidences. They believe God created the universe and everything in it, but cannot perform miracles. Some of them believe that, when God was finished creating, He considered His work finished, backed off and left people to fend for themselves.

Lloyd contradicted those therapists. "I thank my God for allowing the stroke to happen to me," he told them. "Yes, I'm in a wheelchair, but I don't expect to be there a whole lot longer. Remember, when you're in the middle of adversity, seek God with diligence. Don't ask Him why; ask Him why not."

Leaving them to ponder that, Lloyd pauses momentarily and then tells them he's not quitting his therapy because he's preparing for rain. And, when they give him a puzzled look, Lloyd proceeds to tell them Jesus' story about the two farmers who prayed for rain. They desperately needed it because of the severe drought they were going through, and it was the season for planting.

"One farmer thought about it and then went out and planted seeds in his field. The other farmer also thought about it and decided it would be wiser to wait for rain. So, which one had faith that God was going to deliver rain? Some will say the one who held back. The correct one was the farmer who went ahead and planted the seeds.

I'm not walking the way I used to normally," Lloyd said. "But I'm preparing for rain. I get up in the morning and exercise, and my walking is getting better and better. I go to therapy every Tuesday and Friday."

When asked if they know where they're going when they die, those who don't know the Lord say they don't know, or nobody knows, or how should I know. Preparing for rain means that, if you don't know where you're going after death, you had better prepare. Because, if you don't, like Lloyd's stroke, which happened without warning and could have killed him where he fell, you may miss the bus that goes to heaven. If you haven't given your life to Jesus, wherever you are, whatever you're doing, stop. Now is the time. You may not get another chance. John 3:16 tells you how to get the ticket. Grab it, because then you'll know where you're going before the next lightning bold hits.

As Lloyd continued his therapy, he met a therapist at the gym in Becker who was fairly new. When Lloyd was wheeled into the room, he noticed people setting up an obstacle course and wondered about its purpose.

"What's going on?" he asked one of the men who was working on setting it up. As he was finishing with adjusting the spacing, he introduced himself to Lloyd and told him it was an exercise in walking and strengthening his legs.

"The idea is to weave in and out of the course without knocking anything over. Do you want to try it?"

"Sure," said Lloyd, who was always up for a challenge.

"As you probably know, the belt is used in the medical field for safety reasons when helping patients in and out of wheelchairs," the therapist said, as he grabbed a wide belt and fastened it around Lloyd's waist. "I'll be right behind you. keeping a loose hold on you just in case you become a little unsteady. If you want to stop, let me know, and I'll help you to your wheelchair."

"The first time I tried it, I didn't knock anything over. Then they changed the course a little and had me try it again. Every time I did well, they changed things to make it more challenging. And, I liked that. It was a lot of fun."

Next, the therapist timed him as he went through the course, and it took Lloyd two minutes 36 seconds to get to the end and back. "So, he asked me if I wanted to do it again, and I said,

'Absolutely. Let's do it.' So, we went through the same obstacle course again, and we turned around and went back, taking a full minute less than the first time."

Another part of his therapy was to walk around the perimeter of the clinic and see how far he could go in six minutes. "I could do 300 feet in six minutes," Lloyd said. "Then, after a second test weeks later, I went 350 feet. So that was a big jump."

When Lloyd had therapy, which was twice a week, he worked hard. "As I keep working at strengthening my legs, I need to work at getting my left leg to push the same as the right leg pushes. And, I'm handling that pretty well. So, I'm beating those times," he told his sister.

"Well, keep going," she said. "Maybe the next time I talk to you, you'll be taking some steps on your own."

At first when Lloyd began attending church, people swarmed around him because they had missed him. To them, it was the return of a soldier who just returned from a long battle with an enemy bent on killing him. This was the man they had prayed for in his absence and now were eager to hear the story of his survival and the miracles that made it happen. He had answers for all of them, and they were pleased that God had listened to the many people who had been praying for him and requested that he be healed.

"If God had wanted us to go through the challenge of diversities," Lloyd advised his friends, "He would want us to go through them with courage and to learn from them. And I have been learning from all of this. About increasing in faith, learning about listening to God, about talking to Jesus, reading his Word, and ministering to others. That's the statement God gave me; to go through the stroke and the effects of it with His grace and courage."

One day, a young man in church walked up to him and asked,

"Haven't you ever felt angry with God or depressed over your condition? Especially when you were helpless and couldn't do anything for yourself?" It was a question Lloyd expected because most people would have reacted that way.

"It's been difficult and challenging," Lloyd said. "In spite of it, I have not felt sorry for myself nor felt angry or depressed, which are all the things we're supposed to feel according to the world. But what good would that do? Instead, I felt at peace and I had joy. I realized my faith in God was getting stronger as I walked through this journey."

"Do you ever get frustrated because you might not be progressing as fast as you expected?" someone else asked.

"Whenever I feel that way, I pray about it. And because of my faith, God takes care of it," Loyd answered.

"I know He would never let anything happen to His adopted kids unless it's for their best or for people around them," he said. "So, after I was home, when I did happen to space out in the garage and cut my head and dislocated my hip, I thought for a second, 'Why would God allow me to fall like that?' And then, it hit me; that I might have been coming along too quick and needed to slow down."

When it happened, Vicki, the fear of another stroke still fresh on her mind, immediately called an ambulance. The EMTs checked Lloyd for injuries and figured if he had any, they were minor. In spite of what they said, Vicki insisted they take him to the hospital to be checked by a doctor. An MRI showed no broken bones, and no stroke, but he complained that his hip popped every time he tried to use his left leg.

"That made me uneasy," Lloyd said. "But with some specialized exercises, it kept getting better."

One day, after he was home, Vicki asked out of curiosity, "Lloyd why do you think God did this (the stroke) to you?"

Lloyd looked at her and asked, "Why not? Perhaps it was because I had a lot of learning to do. And He had to do what was necessary to get my attention, as hard-headed as I was." After pausing for a second, he told her, "It seemed fair to me."

Vicki had no response, just looked at him in amazement, sensing he had more to say. So, he went on to explain. "Understand, when you become a born-again Christian, it doesn't absolve all problems or adversity. I know our government has screwed up. But, because I cannot walk or fight, I should be worried out of my mind for my family. But God has said He's taking care of us. We need to take a look at God's Word and pray, because He's in control of everything.

If being a believer meant we'd have no adversities, why would Jesus say, '*In this world you will have trouble. But take heart! I, Jesus, have overcome the world (with my death and resurrection).' John 16:33.*

And that gives me all the hope I could possibly think of. My God walks with us every day, all day and keeps us safe every night. He's taking care of us. Those who believe in Him are His children."

There are some Bible verses Lloyd says he not only reads, but studies as well, Lloyd told some of his visitors. "And they're all about God taking care of us. What's happening today is for the good of us and the country. The Lord has directed me, and I believe He has been for a long time, to get more and deeper into prayer and praying for other people as well."

After his stroke, Lloyd began a prayer journal. "Because I tend to forget names, at all times, I carry a small tablet and something to write with in my shirt so I can write down the names of people who want and need prayer. I call that my brain so I don't forget to put those requests in my journal. And as I'm reading God's Word every day, the Holy Spirit will bring to me a verse meant for a certain person He wants me to pray for. And, I do that.

12

PRAISE GOD

The Lord is my shepherd, I shall not want. He
makes me lie down in green pastures. He leads me
beside quiet waters. He restores my soul.

PSALM 23.

The doctor was right when he said Lloyd's recovery would be a long difficult journey with no promise of total recovery. In spite of being told that, Lloyd chose to take the challenge to stay on Earth when he could have chosen the easy way and gone with Jesus. But as he traveled, when facing a boulder blocking the road, he never gave up in spite of doctors who advised him that he wouldn't complete the journey, the end of which led to walking.

In spite of what he was told, he said, "I really do enjoy taking that opportunity (to stay alive). And I praise God that he stepped in and intervened, that He did give me a choice. When I pray, I thank God for everything; my family, my church, our house, the car, therapy every day. The Bible says, this is the day the Lord hath made. He told us to 'be glad and rejoice in it.' Because there may not be another."

Everyone who finds themselves in difficult situations reacts to them differently. Some handle it by going deep into depression. Others find ways to cope. Still others, like Lloyd, accept whatever it is and go to God for help. Those who don't know the Lord, often turn bitter when things go bad, rejecting those around them, blaming God, asking Him angrily why He did this to them.

Perhaps they didn't see the boulder in the middle of the road, stumbled into it and gave up. Perhaps, the boulder was God's way of sending them a message, trying to get their attention. Perhaps if they went to Him in prayer, He would remove the boulder from their path or help them get around it. One can only guess the reasons He may have for allowing things to turn bad instead of intervening for the better.

Lloyd never worried about his situation because he knew God was right beside him, urging him on with every step no matter how much difficulty or pain it would cost him. It reminded him of two men who loved their God so much that, though they were going through terrible times, never gave up their trust in Him.

The first was Job, who was a righteous man. The devil made a bet with God that he could make Job curse him and worship Satan. Of course, God took the bet. So, the devil tortured Job, day and night with excruciating bodily pain and other maladies that seemingly had no end and eventually caused his wife and friends to turn away from him. Though he was advised by his wife and Satan to end his misery by cursing God and worshiping Satan, Job continued to worship the God he loved and trusted, figuring He had a good reason for allowing his misery.

The second man was Horatio Spafford, who had arranged a family vacation across the ocean. Horatio, who worked for the Presbyterian Church, had some important last-minute work to do before departure. So, he sent his wife and four daughters ahead, thinking he would meet them when his work was finished. But he never made it. His family was on their way home when their ocean liner was rammed by a British vessel.

The vessel sank quickly, drowning his four daughters. Only his wife survived, but barely. Though he was suffering overwhelming grief and guilt for the loss of his daughters, he sat down and wrote the words to the well-known hymn *It is Well with My Soul*. It was well with his soul because he believed in and trusted God, knowing He had a purpose for him. And with that faith and trust, he was able to walk on and rebuild his life.

It's incomprehensible how, in less than a heartbeat, a person's life can change one way or another. Following Lloyd's stroke, his family was overwhelmed, which was understandable because it happened so fast and unexpectedly. And, though they would have given their lives to help him, there was nothing they could do.

It was as though God were telling them, "I know you want to help and that it won't be easy for you to stand aside, but Lloyd will have to do this on his own."

With all that Lloyd was going through, his family and church were supportive and showed him how much they cared by visiting him, praying with him each time. Because most of them had jobs and families, it wasn't always easy for them to get there. And Lloyd recognized that.

He also knew they did their best because, right then, he was a priority in their lives, a priority they didn't want to lose. Their visits raised his spirits as he traveled the long and sometimes lonely road to recovery separated for two years from family, friends, and church. He appreciated their support and prayed for them as well because they were his guardian angels.

"As we walked through these times, long days, long nights and months, and now we're into two years, we realize there is recovery," Vicki told a friend who had been praying for them. Along the way, for Lloyd and his family, it was like trying to push the boulder off the road with one hand. But no matter how difficult the journey was, he kept trudging on with Jesus at his side.

"He's worked very hard to get where he is," she told her friend. "We've had miracles happen before our eyes. And we continue to see that. Sure, we have setbacks. So, we continue to pray as we walk through them. Before the stroke, he used to say he was strong as a bull. And I think that continues to be something we all smile about when I ask him how he is doing and he says 'strong like a bull.'"

Now, in 2024, Lloyd continues to go to church, never missing a Sunday unless deep snow shuts down the roads or he is ill. His wife drives him, pulling into the handicap parking next to the entrance. Once parked, she goes to the car's passenger side and waits for someone to bring the wheelchair from the church and set it next to the car door.

With the wheelchair in place and locked, Lloyd moves off the seat, steps onto the ground, turns around, and with someone standing beside him, sits down. From there, he is wheeled into the building. If there isn't someone available right away to push him into the sanctuary, he does it on his own by scooting the wheelchair ahead with both legs. After gaining feeling in his left leg, Lloyd admitted he could walk with someone beside him, but not far. That is, if his equilibrium cooperated.

It took a little more than two years, plenty of help, encouragement from friends and his church, prayer, and miracles along the way to go from being totally helpless, to taking steps. And, he says he's not done yet. As of early 2024, he still does therapy at home and at the gym and thanks God daily for the ability. It was a long two-year endurance trip, but he proved that, with Jesus in the room, he could do it.

"We're grateful and thankful for all the people who have prayed for us," Vicki said. "The people at church, our prayer team, and Pastor and his family who were helping us around the clock with everything. So, that made a big difference with everything going on. Not that we would depend on people to lift us up."

"Our pastor visited me at St. Ben's and prayed for me every week since the beginning of my stroke," Lloyd said. "He told me everyone at church was praying for me as well. My family visited me almost every day, some of them three times a day."

Through it all, Lloyd had advice for others. "If you haven't experienced the grace of God and His peace and wisdom through prayer, you must take the opportunity every day to pray in Jesus' name and read His Word every day. Through this whole process, I'm at peace. That doesn't mean I don't get frustrated once in a while. But when it does come, I pray for God to take it away. And He does. I want to have courage through all of this. And that's important to me as well. Being an example for others.

Peace and joy in the blood of Jesus," Lloyd said. "And I don't mention that word the blood lightly. It's important for everyone to know that Jesus had to give everything for you and me. God showed His absolute love for all of us, and His son was a sacrifice for our sins. The life on this earth we live, we live because of Jesus. And if we don't, we're the ones who end up losing."

Because she was his caretaker during the time of his hospitalization and recovery and saw him often, Christie got to know Lloyd well.

When he was home again, she wrote: "As I have walked Lloyd toward his recovery after his stroke, I have seen clear answers and hope endure. Lloyd not only shares a love for Jesus, but because of his overflowing love, he also shares a deep love for his family, sister, and community. Lloyd continues to inspire others to press on and to always press in to Jesus."

Love the Lord your God with all your heart, and with all your soul, and with all your strength. Dt 6:5.

God bless you all.

13

WHO GOD IS

God is described as Wonderful, Counciler, Almighty God, Everlasting Father, Prince of Peace. He is Father of the Trinity: Father, Son, Holy Spirit. We pray to God, but we end our prayers by saying, "In the name of Jesus, Amen." This is because Jesus says, *John 14:5; Jesus said "I am the way and the truth, and the life. No one comes to the father except through me."*

Wonderful: He is unconditional love. He is truth, grace, and forgiveness. He laughs with you, and has a sense of humor. He also cries with you, listens to your prayers, and answers them. He will walk you through your darkest days. The beauty of His creation surrounds us. It's His gift to us. *John 3:16; For God so loved the world that He gave His only begotten son that whoever believes in Him shall not parish but have eternal life.*

Counciler: Go to Him with your problems. He will listen to you and understand. He will guide you through them, advise you, and send you off on the right path. *Psalm 23:3; He guides me along the right paths for His name's sake.*

Almighty God: He is the Master Creator of all that exists:

John:1-5; In the beginning was the Word, and the Word was with God, and the Word was God. He was with God in the beginning. Through Him all things were made that has been made. In Him was life, and that life was the light of all mankind. The light shines in the darkness, and the darkness has not overcome it.

He has the power to heal, power over governments, over wars and countries, and power over Satan, who will eventually be eliminated. He punishes wrong doing and rewards righteousness. Nothing escapes Him. He knows everything including the hearts, thoughts and actions of every person on Earth. There is no hiding from Him. And all of it is in His hands.

Everlasting Father: His wisdom is infinite, and as such, He is to be obeyed, respected, and trusted. His love, grace, and forgiveness are never ending. He is forever. He is the way, the truth, and the life. *Revelation 22:13; I am the Alpha and the Omega, the First and the Last, the beginning and the end.*

Prince of Peace: When Jesus returns as King, Satan will be eliminated, and there will be peace on Earth through Jesus, the Prince of Peace. Peace God had planned from the beginning but that was lost due to free will and the sins of humanity.

God's Word:

The Bible should on be top of your must-read list of books, because it's the most important book you'll ever read. It was used by America's founders to shape our country; they created our laws from what the Bible says about punishing crime, judges, and fairness.

The Bible teaches us many things including: how to live, how to treat others, love and friendship, being givers instead of takers, how to solve problems, how to pray, and handle adversities. It's about marriage, how to raise children; it talks about Satan, his purposes, how to avoid being caught in his snare by living in Christ; the end times, what to expect so we can be aware and know how to get through them. And there is much more.

As Lloyd says, living in Jesus will save you. Go to Him in prayer, always.

14

THE MIRACLES

DEFINITION OF A MIRACLE

Merriam Webster defines miracles as: 1. *an extraordinary event manifesting divine intervention in human affairs; 2. an extremely outstanding or unusual event, thing or accomplishment; 3. a divinely natural phenomenon experienced humanly as the fulfillment of spiritual law.*

People may wonder why God allowed Lloyd to suffer a stroke causing paralyses. Did He allow it or did He purposely cause it to get his attention, as in the story of Job? This was not just an ordinary stroke fixable by surgery, one that most people would survive. It was one where the odds of survival were almost nil, a stroke that left him helpless, totally dependent, minutes away from death, and in need of many miracles to survive.

Some people might wonder why, if God is all knowing and knew what was going to happen, He allowed it. In Lloyd's thinking, it was a blessing because he was chosen for a mission. And God, knowing Lloyd was a righteous man, would witness to others about His glory, and how non-believers could ready themselves to join God's kingdom. It also allowed Lloyd to talk about the many miracles God would perform to convince unbelievers who He is.

THE MIRACLES

The first miracle happened at the super market where, unknowingly, the vessels in Lloyd's brain were stretching and weakening. No one suspected it, though his speech wasn't quite normal. The miracle is that God prevented the vessels from breaking in the supermarket or in his vehicle on the way to the gym.

The second miracle was that the vessels broke at the gym where the workers immediately recognized what it was, the urgency for getting help, and knew how to respond.

The next miracle was, when Lloyd's daughter, Katie, upon driving toward home from work the afternoon of the stroke, turned down the street leading to the gym instead of to her home. She saw her father's vehicle in the parking lot and the ambulance in front of the gym and decided to stop. This one could be attributed to the Holy Spirit.

The doctors said there was a strong possibility Lloyd wasn't going to survive and advised his family to be prepared to let him go. After Lloyd saw Jesus in the room (another miracle) and told Him he wanted to live, another scan showed the bleeding had stopped, which meant chances of healing and no further paralysis.

When Lloyd began therapy, he asked God for Christian therapists, and God answered his prayers several times by surrounding him with doctors, nurses, and therapists who were believers in Jesus.

Lloyd almost had to be sent home when their insurance coverage was ending, and Vicki didn't know what to do. After much work and frustration, she received a call an hour before Lloyd's release, that God had solved the problem for them.

A nurse who attended Lloyd's church was told by the Holy Spirit that she was chosen to take care of Lloyd.

Through therapy, Lloyd recovered feeling and use of his paralyzed leg and partial use of his left arm.

Lloyd began this journey with paralysis on his whole left side, and in a couple of years, with much work and help from God, he progressed to walking a short distance with help and the hope of walking by himself.

The Hemorrhagic stroke caused severe paralysis on the left side of Lloyd's body including the part of his head that controls speech and can affect one's ability to communicate. For some people who have similar strokes, the damage is severe and permanent. Though Lloyd's speech was slightly affected, with minimal therapy and the grace of God, his communication abilities quickly returned to normal.

Sometimes it takes a near-death experience to wake us up to the miracles and blessings that surround us daily: all of creation; the joining of a tiny egg and sperm that produces another human being or animal; a beautiful flower that grows into a fruit or vegetable that will sustain us; a colorful rainbow, sunset or sunrise (smiles from God); hollow hairs in a horse's coat that insulates and keeps him warm in the winter; the human body and brain designed to operate like a well-oiled machine; trees and other growing things that give us oxygen in return for our exhaled carbon dioxide; and much more; all things created in detail by a Master Artist unequaled by anything humans are able to accomplish.

Printed in the United States
by Baker & Taylor Publisher Services